797,885 Books
are available to read at

www.ForgottenBooks.com

Forgotten Books' App
Available for mobile, tablet & eReader

ISBN 978-1-330-88790-5
PIBN 10117367

This book is a reproduction of an important historical work. Forgotten Books uses state-of-the-art technology to digitally reconstruct the work, preserving the original format whilst repairing imperfections present in the aged copy. In rare cases, an imperfection in the original, such as a blemish or missing page, may be replicated in our edition. We do, however, repair the vast majority of imperfections successfully; any imperfections that remain are intentionally left to preserve the state of such historical works.

Forgotten Books is a registered trademark of FB &c Ltd.
Copyright © 2017 FB &c Ltd.
FB &c Ltd, Dalton House, 60 Windsor Avenue, London, SW19 2RR.
Company number 08720141. Registered in England and Wales.

For support please visit www.forgottenbooks.com

1 MONTH OF
FREE
READING

at
www.ForgottenBooks.com

By purchasing this book you are eligible for one month membership to ForgottenBooks.com, giving you unlimited access to our entire collection of over 700,000 titles via our web site and mobile apps.

To claim your free month visit:
www.forgottenbooks.com/free117367

* Offer is valid for 45 days from date of purchase. Terms and conditions apply.

English
Français
Deutsche
Italiano
Español
Português

www.forgottenbooks.com

Mythology Photography **Fiction** Fishing Christianity **Art** Cooking Essays Buddhism Freemasonry Medicine **Biology** Music **Ancient Egypt** Evolution Carpentry Physics Dance Geology **Mathematics** Fitness Shakespeare **Folklore** Yoga Marketing **Confidence** Immortality Biographies Poetry **Psychology** Witchcraft Electronics Chemistry History **Law** Accounting **Philosophy** Anthropology Alchemy Drama Quantum Mechanics Atheism Sexual Health **Ancient History Entrepreneurship** Languages Sport Paleontology Needlework Islam **Metaphysics** Investment Archaeology Parenting Statistics Criminology **Motivational**

HISTORIC
CLAREMONT
NEW YORK

"THE WARMEST
WELCOME OF
AN INN"

LOOKING UP THE HUDSON FROM GRANT'S TOMB

ILLUSTRATING VARIOUS INCIDENTS
AND PLACES ROUND ABOUT
HISTORIC CLAREMONT
CLAREMONT HEIGHTS
RIVERSIDE DRIVE, NEW YORK CITY

F128
.8
.C59C5

*Especially Arranged
Executed and
Copyrighted by*
Chasmar-Winchell Press
1907

Along in the Early Days
1609

IN the twilight of a September evening, nearly three hundred years ago, came Hudson's good ship the "Half Moon," to "a very good land to fall in with, and a pleasant land to see," as its commander refers to it in the log.

This same quaint old log-book of the "Half Moon" describes the land as "very high and mountainous" and the river as "full of fish." It speaks of "very loving people and very old men," and of "a house constructed of oak bark and circular in shape, so that it had the appearance of being built with an arched roof."

"The land," says Hudson, "is the finest for cultivation that I ever in my life set foot upon, and it also abounds in trees of every description. The natives are very good people, for when they saw that I would not remain, they supposed I was afraid of their bows, and taking the arrows they broke them in pieces and threw them in the fire." Such were the evidences of hospitality three hundred years ago, and on the crest of one of the wooded hills, two leagues from the mouth of the river and on the right bank, stands a hostelry where guests are to-day as warmly welcomed, if not in the same manner.

1609—HENDRICK HUDSON'S "HALF MOON"

1 6 0 9

"THE end for shipping to go" was the report of the small boat expedition sent ahead of the "Half Moon"; and the log continues, "for they had been up eight or nine leagues and found but seven foot water and unconstant soundings." The little high pooped, flat bottomed Dutch yacht and its daring commander had failed in their mission; the passage to India and the east, the search for which had lured Columbus onto the unknown sea a century before, was still unfound.

1776—BATTLE OF HARLEM HEIGHTS

1 7 7 6

THIS historic year witnessed the Battle of Harlem Heights. The British troops were gathered on Claremont Hill. Across the "Hollow way," now partly spanned by the viaduct, were the Americans. The derisive notes of a fox horn floated across to the "rebel" lines; the game was run to cover. But Knowlton and his rangers were flanking the British, skirting along what is now Broadway, and Nixon with 150 men was tempting the redcoats into the Hollow. The fox turned, and the day was won for freedom.

1807—FIRST TRIP OF FULTON'S "CLERMONT"

1 8 0 7

THE paddle, the wind, and then—steam. It was thought ridiculous when Fulton and Chancellor Livingston applied to the New York State legislature for exclusive right to navigate the waters of the state by steam, and the tenure would probably have been made for a hundred years with as little thought as it was then made for twenty. "Fulton's folly," they called it, but the little "Clermont" steamed from New York, passing those on Claremont Hill who believed in her, fled from on all sides by superstitious boatmen, and reached Albany in thirty-two hours.

1856—CLAREMONT AS A ROADHOUSE.—From a Photograph

1 8 5 6

IT was in this year that Claremont became a famous roadhouse with one Edmund Jones as proprietor, and the reign of public hospitality then began. Southward stretched the fine Dutch farms and the wheat fields which saw the finish of the Battle of Harlem Heights. For many years a private residence, Claremont first became historic in 1816 through its occupancy by Joseph Bonaparte, ex-king of Spain and brother to the great Napoleon. We may be sure that he counted among his visitors, Louis Philippe, Lafayette, and Talleyrand, who were frequent guests at the Jumel mansion nearby.

The Garden

THE historic associations of Claremont are not memories only. A few steps to the south, the east or the north bring us to still standing monuments of the history of our country. The Hudson still sweeps past the high hill crowned by historic Claremont, but the "Hollow way" is in part spanned by the great viaduct. Beyond this still stands the historic Jumel mansion on 161st Street east of St. Nicholas Avenue. Coming south along "the lane," now Broadway and Claremont Avenue, through which the British chased Reed and Knowlton in the first skirmish of the Battle of Harlem Heights, we come to the still uncut "Point of Rocks" at 127th Street and Convent Avenue, from which Washington and his generals watched the battle. Lower down by a few blocks stands Columbia University, dating from 1746. At 110th Street and Morningside Heights stands the slowly growing arch of the great cathedral of St. John the Divine, and still farther south and west stretches Riverside Drive, with the Soldiers' and Sailors' Monument at 89th Street and some of the most beautiful houses of the city. Thus are memories of the past combined with the promises of the future.

THE LIBRARY, COLUMBIA UNIVERSITY

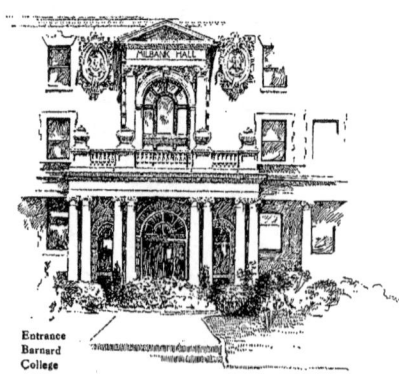

Entrance
Barnard
College

COLUMBIA had its inception in a lottery, the holding of which Governor Clinton authorized in 1746. Eight years later Dr. Samuel Johnson, of Stratford, Connecticut, was called to the presidency of "King's College," as it was then known, and on ground at Park Place and West Broadway given by the Corporation of Trinity Church, the great work began. The institution moved to its present location in 1897. To-day its grounds extend over six city blocks, its buildings include the beautiful domed Library, halls for both collegiate and university studies, and the newly built Dormitories. West of Columbia lies Barnard College, which stands among the foremost of educational institutions for women.

SOLDIERS' AND SAILORS' MONUMENT

RIVERSIDE PARK, which fittingly crowns the right bank of the Hudson, is distinguished by two unusual structures, Grant's Tomb and the Soldiers' and Sailors' Monument. The latter, at 89th Street, was erected in 1902 to the memory of the brave Union men who died in the Civil War. The approach, the great bronze based flagpole, and the hundred foot monument itself form a fitting memorial. To the north and south stretches the drive with its palatial mansions, that of Mr. Charles M. Schwab at 73d Street being the only residence in the city which occupies an entire block.

Residence
Mr. Chas. M. Schwab

CATHEDRAL OF ST. JOHN THE DIVINE

Chapel
Columbia
University

LOOKING east from Broadway, at 112th Street may be seen one of the great supporting arches of the new Episcopal Cathedral, the cornerstone of which was laid in 1892. The final cost of the work has been estimated at ten million dollars, and the time required to finish it, a century. The structure crowns Morningside Heights, alluded to by ex-Mayor Low as "The Acropolis of the New World." In contrast to the vast pile in size, if not in beauty, is the newly built St. Paul's Chapel of Columbia University on Amsterdam Avenue east of the library. Seating nearly a thousand persons, the Chapel conforms in size and architectural treatment to the surrounding buildings.

THE JUMEL MANSION

In Revolutionary Days

THE Jumel Mansion is one of the most interesting historic houses of the city. Built in 1758 by Roger Morris, Esq., its royalist owner lost possession of his estates during the Revolution, and the house was used as Washington's Headquarters, and later was the home of Aaron Burr. In 1810 it became the property of Stephen Jumel, and in those days of social renaissance saw royalty among its guests. The Jumels added to its furniture specimens from the Tuileries which had been owned by Napoleon. To-day the house, recently acquired by the City, has been turned over to the Daughters of the American Revolution, and is the depository of many historic relics.

Claremont of To-Day

East Front

IVERSIDE DRIVE sweeps northward, with its spreading trees and its ample walks and bridle path, past Grant's Tomb to Claremont. The house stands on a beautiful sweep of high land, just north of the tomb, nestled among the great elms on the hilltop. One enters first the central room and office, with its heavy furniture and decorations of great antlers, and various relics and old prints of both former and more recent historic times. The piazza encircles the house, and either there or in the gardens may be put to the test "The warmest welcome of an Inn."

The view to the north comprehends the whole sweep of the Hudson and the lordly Palisades. The house faces the wooded Jersey shore, while to the south beyond the garden rises Grant's Tomb, and the Hudson is visible almost in the whole of its course down past the city. Claremont is visited daily by hundreds who stop either for a glimpse of history or for refreshment. The cuisine is unsurpassed; live trout are brought direct from the hatcheries and kept in the fountain in the garden. During the shad season, Claremont sets its own nets in the river just at hand.

HE white granite tomb of General Ulysses S. Grant, 160 feet in height and 300 feet above the surface of the Hudson, is just south of Claremont. It was constructed at a cost of $600,000 and dedicated in 1897. The body of the famous general, which had for several years rested in a small, temporary structure on the hillside just at hand, found a final resting place in one of the twin sarcophagi in the crypt, and not many years after the body of his wife was placed beside him.

The one-time Chinese Ambassador to the United States, Li Hung Chang, contributed a mark of interest to this historic spot. Directly behind the tomb stands a tree which he planted in 1897 to the memory of the American hero, and a bronze tablet bears in Chinese and English his tribute to General Grant.

The tomb stands upon historic ground, and it seems most fitting that it should stand where, during revolutionary times, our forefathers sowed the seed of the Union, winning on this very spot the Battle of Harlem Heights. At that time there stood upon this exact location the country residence of one George Pollock, to which he gave the name of Monte Alta; and close at hand was entombed the body of one of his children. The little fenced in monument bears the inscription: "Erected to the memory of an amiable child, St. Claire Pollock. Died 15 July, 1797, in the fifth year of his age."

Tomb of "An Amiable Child"

GRANT'S TOMB, RIVERSIDE DRIVE

HE gardens of Claremont are the pride of the city. They offer opportunity for rest and refreshment, whether it be for the party "en route" for the open country north of the city or for the formal and elaborate dinner. Here have been enjoyed many private social functions, receptions, wedding breakfasts and kindred entertainments, and there are many prominent in the social, financial, naval, military and diplomatic world who have been glad to avail themselves of the unique facilities which the house, the grounds and the management, afford to all who seek the hospitality of Claremont.

The old world abounds in the out-of-door places of a similar nature, where rest and refreshment may be had in an environment close to nature, but there is probably no other place in the world where a majestic river, a picture shore-line, landscape gardening, beautiful trees and velvety lawns combine with all that inner man can suggest.

Claremont has often been the scene of municipal entertainment. In 1897 a luncheon was given to President McKinley and five hundred guests; in 1899 a breakfast to Admiral Dewey and four hundred guests. On this latter occasion the menu, linen, silver and china bore a special coat of arms combining the word "Claremont" with the seal of the City and the four stars betokening the rank of Admiral, and is still in use as the emblem of Claremont.

The Hendrick Hudson

UNDER THE ELMS AT CLAREMONT

Under the spreading elms of the west garden, the view is unsurpassed. The air sweeps up from the river and is always refreshing. The "bite to eat" is here served in the open beside the splashing fountain, and with all the care and daintiness that distinguishes the hospitality of "Historic Claremont."

THE interior decorations of Claremont are of unusual interest. The mural treatment lends itself to the varied collection of pewter, brass and pottery. Particular attention is called to the unique collection of etchings by W. Dendy Sadler and Herbert Dicksee. Those by the former artist form a complete collection of his work, depicting for the most part domestic scenes in Old England, while the Dicksee collection, depicting dogs and children, is one of the few complete collections in America. The etchings are tastefully disposed throughout the entire house and particularly on the stairway. There are also many examples of furniture of those good old days of our forefathers, when honest labor combined with an artistic sense in examples which have outlived their makers.

The ground floor and piazza offer facilities for the entertainment of the public, while private parties may find on the upper floors small dining rooms decorated to accord with certain periods or types. The Mission Reading Room, opening on the stairway, contains books of a nature appropriate to the historic associations of the place, and from this room opens the west upper veranda. Turn where you will, the picture is never twice alike; indoors decorative attractions galore, and out of doors, the beauty of the place itself, particularly late in the afternoon, as the sun sinking behind the Palisades, lengthens the shadows on the landscape. The outlook from every point is unusually attractive.

A Corner of the Garden

THE COLONIAL GARDEN AT CLAREMONT

The Colonial Garden at Claremont is unique. In it are thirteen tiny shelters, each named after one of the original states. They vary in size to correspond to the relative sizes of the states. Pennsylvania, the Keystone State, is represented by the arch and surrounding ground at the end of the garden, which extends to the grounds on which Grant's Tomb is located.

LAREMONT by night is, if possible, more beautiful than Claremont by day. The view on the opposite page shows the illuminated arch which represents the Keystone State, and beyond the two lines of state shelters stands the house itself evidencing hospitality at every door and window.

The garden is not garishly lighted by electricity, but just sufficiently so to add to and properly set off the color scheme furnished by well gowned women, the beauty of whose costumes is further emphasized by the sober black and white of the evening dress of the men.

From a standpoint of attractiveness, there is little choice between the broad piazzas of the house, and the garden, except that nature furnishes the roof for the latter, but, particularly from the west piazza, perhaps a better view may be had of the surroundings. From this vantage point may be seen the black river, dotted with the twinkling lights of boats at anchor, glide silently by, river steamers come and go, jeweled with lights and sweeping the beams of their searchlights, now upon the great white tomb, now upon the dark woods of the Jersey shore, themselves winking a thousand eyes at the city. Many find rest from the cares of the day by gliding up the stretch of the river drive in silent, wide-eyed automobiles, to stop awhile in the light of Claremont—always awake to the comfort of its guests, always alert to provide something better than others who minister to the public.

A Corner
of the
Verandah

THE GARDEN AT NIGHT

At night the outlook over the river discloses what might properly be called an American Venice. The grim Palisades are topped with a regular line of lights, trolley cars brilliantly lighted appear now and then from among the trees through which the tracks wind, while the view which extends miles in both directions includes the river dotted with stationary and moving lights, and brings to one's mind the thought of that ancient city.

THE COLONIAL ROOM

THE DELFT ROOM

Two private dining rooms of unusual type. The Colonial Room is a model of simplicity and elegance in white and dark green; the Delft Room, typically Dutch, contains many interesting pieces and Dutch scenes and a fine Delft frieze.

THE GOLD ROOM

Claremont
East Entrance

THE WEST VERANDAH

The Gold Room, carpeted in golden brown and replete with Louis XVI furnishings, presents an unusual effect. The verandah view shows it as arranged on the occasion of the Coaching Club luncheon, and illustrates the possibilities at kindred functions.

Proposed Hudson Memorial Bridge at Spuyten Duyvil

CPSIA information can be obtained
at www.ICGtesting.com
Printed in the USA
BVHW041714031218
534659BV00016B/903/P